To

From

Date

T0089558

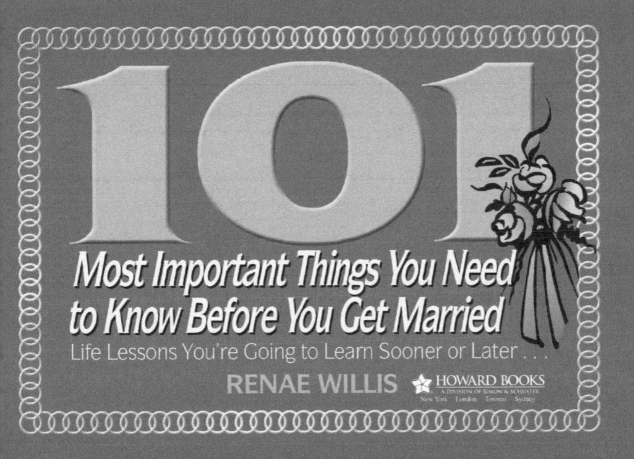

101

Most Important Things You Need to Know Before You Get Married

Life Lessons You're Going to Learn Sooner or Later . . .

RENAE WILLIS

HOWARD BOOKS
A DIVISION OF SIMON & SCHUSTER
New York London Toronto Sydney

Our purpose at Howard Books is to:
Increase faith in the hearts of growing Christians
Inspire holiness in the lives of believers
Instill hope in the hearts of struggling people everywhere
Because He's coming again!

HOWARD
BOOKS

Published by Howard Books, a division of Simon & Schuster, Inc.
1230 Avenue of the Americas, New York, NY 10020
www.howardpublishing.com

101 Most Important Things You Need to Know Before You Get Married © 2008 by Renae Willis

All rights reserved, including the right to reproduce this book or portions thereof in any form whatsoever. For information, address Howard Subsidiary Rights Department, 1230 Avenue of the Americas, New York, NY 10020.

First Howard trade paperback edition February 2008

Library of Congress Cataloging-in-Publication Data
101 most important things you need to know before you get married : life lessons you're going to learn sooner or later— / [compiled by] Renae Willis ; illustrations by Dennis Hill.
   p. cm.
1. Marriage—Quotations, maxims, etc. I. Willis, Renae. II. Title: One hundred one most important things you need to know before you get married. III. Title: One hundred and one most important things you need to know before you get married.
 PN6084.M3A13 2008
 306.81—dc22

2007018546

ISBN 13: 978-1-4165-5010-5
ISBN 10:   1-4165-5010-0

10 9 8 7 6 5 4 3 2 1

HOWARD and colophon are registered trademarks of Simon & Schuster, Inc.

Manufactured in the United States of America

For information regarding special discounts for bulk purchases, please contact: Simon & Schuster Special Sales at 1-800-456-6798 or business@simonandschuster.com.

Edited by Chrys Howard
Cover design by Dennis Hill
Interior design by Tennille Paden
Illustrations by Dennis Hill

Unless otherwise marked all Scripture quotations are taken from the *Holy Bible, New International Version* ®. Copyright © 1973, 1978, 1984 by International Bible Society. Used by permission of Zondervan. All rights reserved. Scripture quotations marked KJV are taken from the *King James Version*. Scripture quotations marked NKJV are taken from the *New King James Version*. Copyright © 1982, 1988 by Thomas Nelson, Inc. All rights reserved. Scripture quotations marked NASB are taken from the *New American Standard Bible*, © 1960, 1962, 1963, 1968, 1971, 1972, 1973, 1975, 1977 by The Lockman Foundation. Used by permission. Scripture quotations marked NLT are taken from the *Holy Bible, New Living Translation*, copyright © 1996. Used by permission of Tyndale House Publishers, Inc., Wheaton, Illinois 60189. All rights reserved. Scripture quotations marked TLB are taken from *The Living Bible*, copyright © 1971. Used by permission of Tyndale House Publishers, Inc., Wheaton, Illinois 60189. All rights reserved.

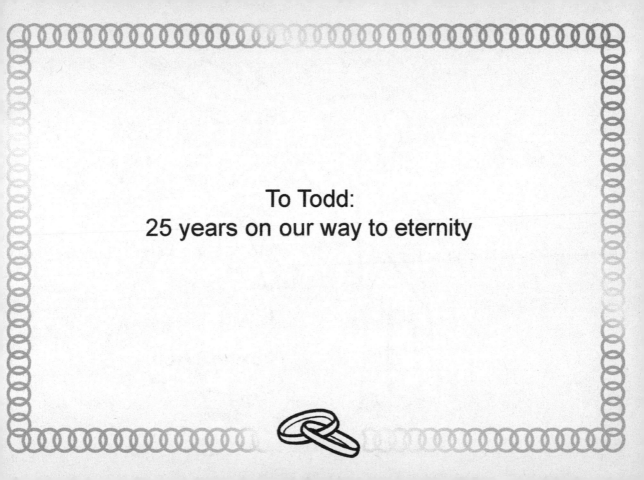

To Todd:
25 years on our way to eternity

1

The secret to a happy marriage is
. . . no secrets.

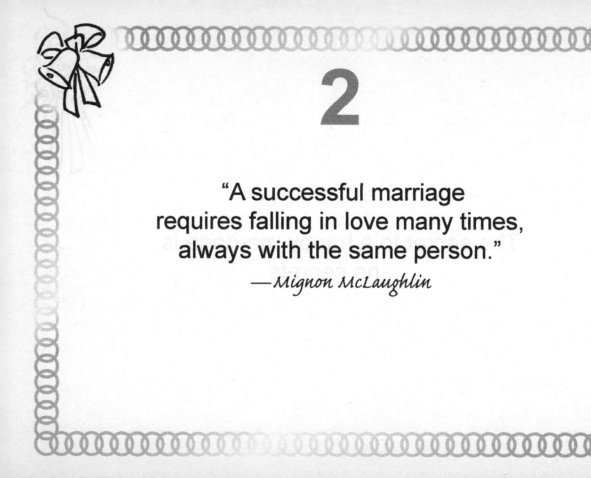

2

"A successful marriage
requires falling in love many times,
always with the same person."

—*Mignon McLaughlin*

3

"One advantage of marriage, it seems to me,
is that when you fall out of love [with
each other], it keeps you together until maybe
you fall in love again."

—*Judith Viorst*

Marriage will be like a roller coaster—
full of ups and downs,
and you'll catch your breath a few times,
but it's definitely a ride worth taking.

4

"Let the wife make the
husband glad to come home,
and let him make her sorry to see him leave."

—*Martin Luther*

*Put your best foot forward for your spouse,
even more than for your friends.*

5

"We come to love not
by finding a perfect person,
but by learning to see
an imperfect person perfectly."

—*Sam Keen*

*No, you are not marrying the perfect person,
but you can love perfectly and,
in that love, make them perfect.*

6

"Sensual pleasures have the
fleeting brilliance of a comet;
a happy marriage
has the tranquility
of a lovely
sunset."

—*Ann Landers*

*Not every day will be full of fireworks,
but every day can be full of love.*

7

"Happy marriages begin when we
marry the ones we love,
and they blossom when we love
the ones we marry."

— *Tom Mullen*

Love is a process that gets better as the years go on.
Be patient and good things will blossom.

8

"There are many things in life
that will catch your eye,
but only a few will catch your heart . . .
pursue those."

— *Tim Redmond*

*"If the grass looks greener on the other side,
it's because they took better care of it."*
—Cecil Selig

9

Love each other always and in all ways.
This sounds simple as you embark
on this journey because you don't know
the "all ways" part yet.
If you truly get
the "always" part,
you'll be fine
with the "all ways."

10

"Get Married.
Stay Married.
What a concept!"
— *The Snipe*

*"The divorce rate would be lower if instead of marrying
for better or worse people would marry for good."*
—Ruby Dee

11

"People shop for a bathing suit with more care
than they do a husband or wife.
The rules are the same. Look for something
you'll feel comfortable wearing.
Allow for room to grow."

—*Erma Bombeck*

12

"I didn't marry you because you were perfect.
I didn't even marry you because I loved you.
I married you because you gave me a promise.
That promise made up for your faults. And the promise I gave
you made up for mine. . . . And when our children were growing
up, it wasn't a house that protected them; and it wasn't our love
that protected them—it was that promise."

— *Thornton Wilder*

*Your marriage vows are not to be thrown away
like yesterday's newspaper. Hold strong to your promises.*

13

"More marriages might survive
if the partners realized that sometimes
the better comes after the worse."

— *Doug Larson*

14

"A good marriage is a contest
of generosity."

—Diane Sawyer

*Give freely of what you have,
give fully of who you are.*

15

"A happy marriage is a long conversation
which always seems too short."

—*Andre Maurois*

*"Being in a long marriage is a little bit like
that nice cup of coffee every morning—
I might have it every day, but I still enjoy it."*
—Steven Gaines

16

If all you've thought
about is the wedding
and not the marriage,
then you may need to think again.

17

"Often the difference between a successful marriage and a mediocre one consists of leaving about three or four things a day unsaid."

—*Harlan Miller*

18

It is easy to make
a mountain out of any molehill.
All you do is add dirt.
Be careful, little mouth,
what you say.

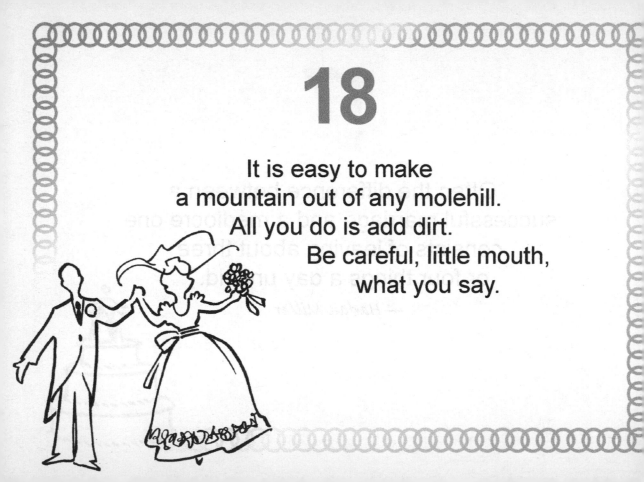

19

"You were united to your wife by the Lord.
In God's wise plan, when you married,
the two of you became one person in his sight."

—*Malachi 2:15* TLB

*Let the love of your life know how special
they are every day.*

20

Marry someone who lifts you up,
not casts you down;
who encourages, not discourages.
Marry for brains, not looks;
marry for love, not lust.

21

"Friendship makes prosperity brighter,
while it lightens adversity by sharing
its griefs and anxieties."

—*Cicero*

*"Shared joy is a double joy;
shared sorrow is half a sorrow."*
—Swedish proverb

22

"God comforts us,
not to make us comfortable,
but to make us comforters."

—*John Henry Jowett*

Few burdens are heavy when both of you are lifting.
Marriage gives you someone with whom to
carry the heavy burdens.

23

"Love is not blind—it sees more,
not less. But because it sees more,
it is willing to see less."

—*Rabbi Julius Gordon*

*Make it a habit to see your partner
as God sees them. God sees all and
loves us anyway.*

24

"I always seek the good that is in people and leave the bad to Him who made mankind and knows how to round off the corners."

—*Goethe's mother*

25

"Be tolerant of the human race.
Your whole family belongs to it—and some of
your spouse's family does too."

—*Author Unknown*

*"Families are like fudge . . .
mostly sweet with a few nuts."*

—Author Unknown

26

"Marriage is not a noun;
it's a verb. It isn't something you get.
It's something you do. It's the way you
love your partner every day."

— *Barbara De Angelis*

*"Marriage is NOT 50/50 . . .
it is 100/100."*

—David J. Stewart

27

"A wedding anniversary is the celebration of love,
trust, partnership, tolerance, and tenacity.
The order varies for any given year."

— *Paul Sweeney*

*Be realistic. A fairy-tale ending
seldom happens, but the alternative
is so much better.*

28

"Marriage is not just spiritual
communion and passionate embraces;
it is also remembering to take out the trash."

— *Dr. Joyce Brothers*

*"No husband was ever shot
while doing the dishes."*

—Author Unknown

29

"Words that soak into your ears
are whispered, not yelled."

—*Author Unknown*

*Warmth, kindness, and a gentle touch
are always stronger than force and fury.*

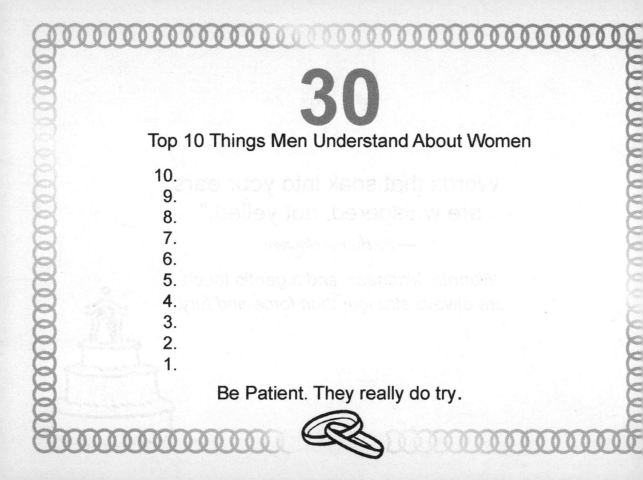

30

Top 10 Things Men Understand About Women

10.
9.
8.
7.
6.
5.
4.
3.
2.
1.

Be Patient. They really do try.

31

"Men are from Earth.
Women are from Earth.
Deal with it."

—George Carlin

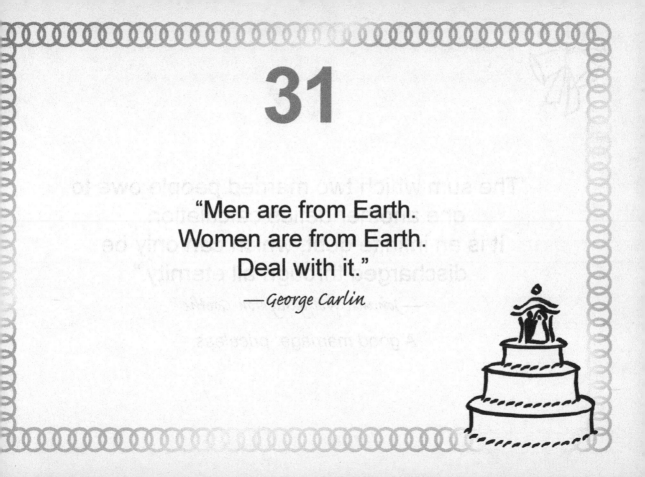

32

"The sum which two married people owe to one another defies calculation.
It is an infinite debt, which can only be discharged through all eternity."

—*Johann Wolfgang von Goethe*

A good marriage: priceless.

33

"Love is the condition
in which the happiness
of another person
is essential to your own."

—*Robert Heinlein*

"*Love seeks not limits,
but outlets.*"
—Author Unknown

34

"Lord, help me to remember the things
I ought not to forget, and to forget the things
I ought not to remember."

—*Author Unknown*

Start each day with a clean slate.

35

"Love doesn't make the world go 'round.
Love is what makes the ride worthwhile."

—*Franklin P. Jones*

*"If I have a faith that can move mountains,
but have not love, I am nothing."*
—1 Corinthians 13:2

36

It's not what you have
in your life that counts,
but who you have
in your life.

37

"Anger makes your mouth
work faster than your brain."

—*Evan Esar*

When one's temper gets the best of us,
it reveals the worst of us.

38

"Always be humble and gentle.
Be patient with each other, making allowance
for each other's faults because of your love.
Make every effort to keep yourselves united
in the Spirit, binding yourselves
together with peace."

—*Ephesians 4:2–3 NLT*

39

"It is only possible
to live happily ever
after on a day-to-day basis."

—*Margaret Bonanno*

*Marriages are made stronger
in spite of circumstances,
not because of them.*

40

"Nothing is so strong as gentleness;
nothing so gentle as real strength."

—*St. Francis de Sales*

*"Out of the overflow of the heart,
the mouth speaks."*
—Matthew 12:34

41

The best marriage is one
where the couple
helps one another to think
the best thoughts,
do the noblest deeds,
and be their finest selves.

42

Opposites may attract,
but it's the similarities you share
that will hold you together in the long run.
Find and hold on to things you
enjoy doing together.

43

"Love at first sight
is easy to understand;
it's when two people
have been looking at each other
for a lifetime that it becomes a miracle."

—*Amy Bloom*

44

"There is nothing nobler or more admirable than when two people who see eye to eye keep house as man and wife, confounding their enemies and delighting their friends."

—*Homer*

Stand together through the trials and joys of life; two are always better than one.

45

"For wherever you go, I will go;
And wherever you lodge, I will lodge;
Your people *shall be* my people.
And your God, my God."

—*Ruth 1:16* NKJV

*Be willing to make sacrifices
for your marriage—even if it means
moving to another city.*

46

"God always gives His very best to those who leave the choice with Him."

—*James Hudson Taylor*

*Ask God's guidance on
all matters of importance.*

47

"Let there be spaces
in your togetherness."
— *Kahlil Gibran*

"Don't smother each other.
No one can grow in shade."
—Leo Buscaglia

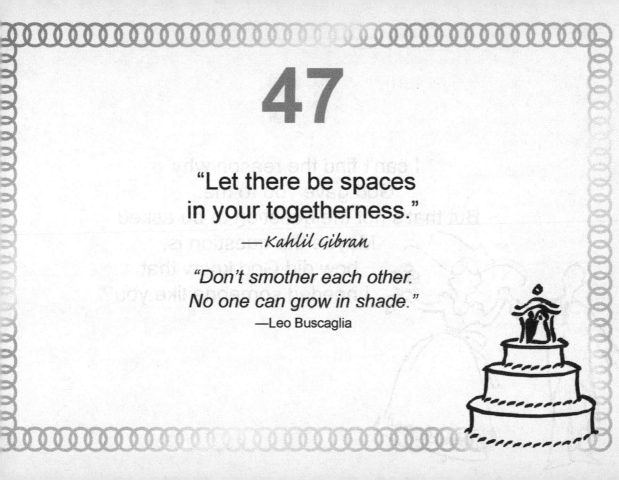

48

I can't find the reason why
God gave you to me.
But that's not the question to be asked.
Maybe the question is,
how did God know that
I needed someone like you?

49

"A happy marriage
is the union of two good forgivers."

—*Robert Quillen*

*It doesn't take
a very big person to
carry even the smallest grudge.*

50

People do not marry people,
not real ones anyway.
They marry who
they think the person is;
they marry illusions and images.
The exciting adventure of marriage
is finding out who the person really is.

51

"Marriage, ultimately,
is the practice of becoming
passionate friends."

—*Harville Hendrix*

*Soul mates aren't found,
they're made.*

52

"One of the great illusions
of our time is that love is self-sustaining.
It is not. Love must be fed and nurtured,
constantly renewed. That demands
ingenuity and consideration,
but first and foremost, it demands time."

—David Mac

53

"You'll want to have lots
of photographs of your wedding
to show to your family and friends,
who will have been unable to see
the actual ceremony
because the photographer
was always in the way."

— *Dave Barry*

54

"Kindness is more than deeds.
It is an attitude, an expression,
a look, a touch. It is anything that
lifts another person."

—*C. Neil Strait*

*When the baby's crying
and the bills are due,
still speak kindly.*

55

"Don't be reckless with
other people's hearts.
And don't put up with people
who are reckless with yours."

—*Mary Schmich*

56

"The time to repair the roof is when the sun is shining."

—*John F. Kennedy*

Don't fight when the tension is already high.
Wait until everyone has calmed down,
then share your concerns.

57

"Except the Lord build the house,
they labour in vain that build it."

— *Psalm 127:1 KJV*

*Make sure your foundation
is strong and the Lord
is the head of your house.
If God's not in it,
it's not worth being in.*

58

Don't marry someone
you hope to change.
If they do change,
it most likely won't be for the better.

59

Make sure that you are the
kind of husband or wife
that you would want
your child to marry.

60

"Any concern too small
to be turned into a prayer
is too small to be made
into a burden."

—Corrie ten Boom

*On a daily basis,
ask the Lord for direction.*

61

"A happy home is more than
a roof over your head—
it's a firm foundation under your feet."

—*Author Unknown*

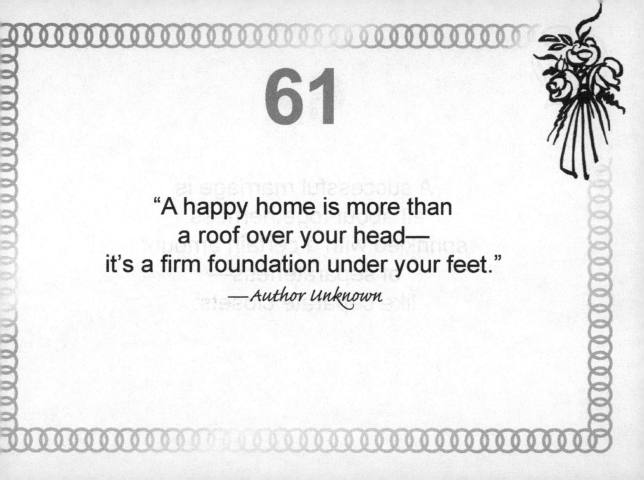

62

A successful marriage is
all about togetherness,
sprinkled with a certain amount
of separateness—
like separate closets.

63

"One good turn
gets most of the blankets."

—*Author Unknown*

64

"Any marriage that survives
a big wedding can probably survive."
—*Malcolm Forbes*

65

Advice for the mother of the bride:
It's her wedding,
not the one you wish you had.

66

In disagreements, fight fairly.
No name-calling and
no dredging up the past.

*Always be prepared
to indulge in a
piece of humble pie.*

67

Whenever you decide
something with an open heart,
you usually make the right decision.
Be willing to listen to the other side.

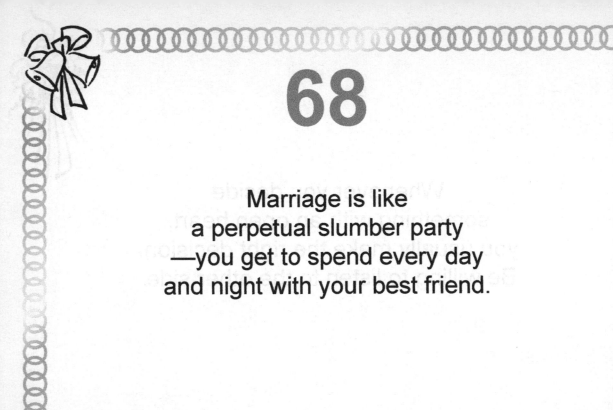

68

Marriage is like
a perpetual slumber party
—you get to spend every day
and night with your best friend.

69

Start each day with a kiss;
end each day with a hug;
and always say,
"I love you,"
whenever you part
from one another.

70

"I have learned,
in whatsoever state I am,
therewith to be content."

— *Philippians 4:11 KJV*

Be happy with yourself first.
Don't expect someone else to
make you happy,
or you never will be.

71

"Real giving is when
we give to our spouses
what's important to them,
whether we understand it, like it,
agree with it, or not."

—*Michele Weiner-Davis*

*This is especially important to
remember around holidays.*

72

Forgive,
forget,
get on with it.

Love does *mean having
to say you're sorry.*

73

Know what you will stand for
and what you won't . . . .
and make sure that you and your partner
are on the same page with this.
You can only know this through communication,
which is the key to a good marriage.

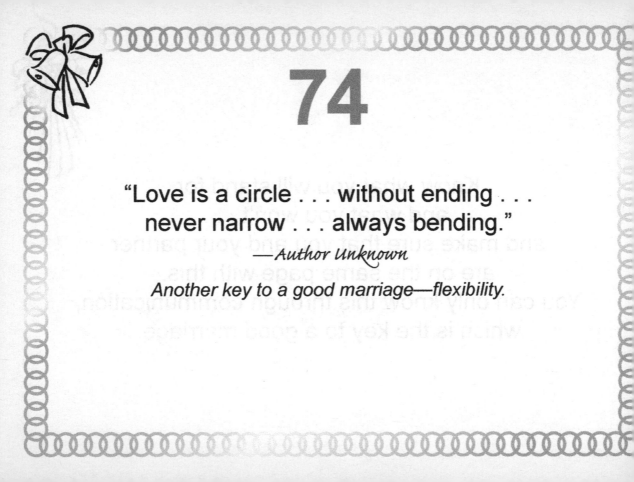

74

"Love is a circle . . . without ending . . .
never narrow . . . always bending."

—*Author Unknown*

Another key to a good marriage—flexibility.

75

Replacing the toilet paper roll
does not cause brain damage.
Neither does unloading
the dishwasher.

76

"The task ahead of us is
never as great as the power behind us."
—*Ralph Waldo Emerson*

*Have a right relationship with
God because He is the source of all love.*

77

Focus on the good
and that's what you'll get.
Good things come in all size packages.
The secret is to open them all
expecting good.

78

"Don't accumulate resentment
until you explode.
Handle and resolve each issue
as it comes up."

—*Bill Turner*

*Wise older couples always say
don't go to bed angry.
They must know
what they're talking about.*

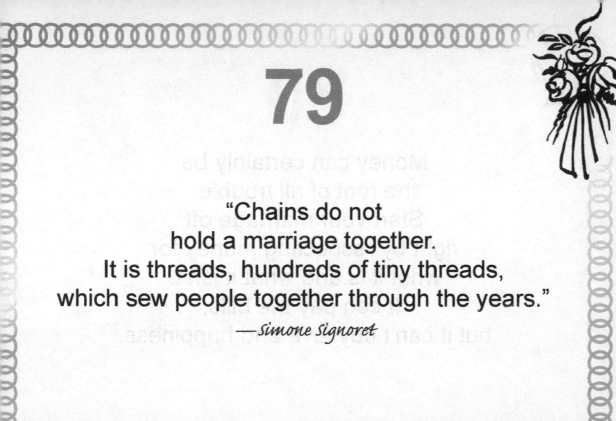

"Chains do not
hold a marriage together.
It is threads, hundreds of tiny threads,
which sew people together through the years."

—*Simone Signoret*

80

Money can certainly be
the root of all trouble.
Start your marriage off
right by respecting money for
what it is and what it isn't.
It can pay the bills,
but it can't buy love and happiness.

81

"The goal in marriage is not to think alike,
but to think together."

—Robert C. Dodds

*Teamwork works in marriages
just as it does in football.
Get a game plan and stick to it.
Everyone's not the quarterback.
It takes all team members
working together for success.*

82

"What counts in making a happy marriage
is not so much how compatible you are,
but how you deal with incompatibility."

—*Author Unknown*

83

Your spouse will not be a mind reader.
If you want your needs met,
then you have to tell him
what they are.

84

"Husbands, love your wives,
just as Christ loved the church
and gave himself up for her."

—*Ephesians 5:25*

*Love means
putting other's
needs before
your own.*

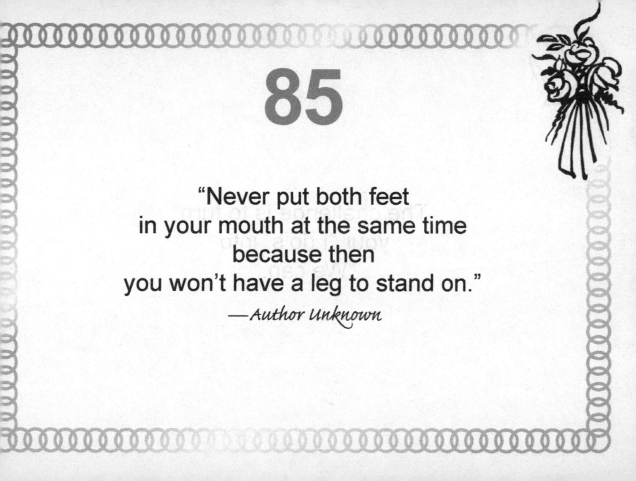

85

"Never put both feet
in your mouth at the same time
because then
you won't have a leg to stand on."

—*Author Unknown*

86

The challenge is to turn
your "I do's" into
"We can."

87

"The entire sum
of existence is the magic
of being needed by
just one person."

—Vi Putnam

88

In every marriage,
it is truly the little things that count.
A cup of coffee, a single rose,
a whispered "I Love You"
will set the tone for a happy day.

89

"Be assured,
if you walk with Him and look to Him,
and expect help from Him,
He will never fail you."

—*George Mueller*

*If God be for our marriage,
who can be against us?*

90

"Perfect love
casts out fear."

—*1 John 4:18* NASB

91

Most days,
about 90 percent of what
happens to you is positive.
Don't take the negative 10 percent
home and dump it on your spouse.

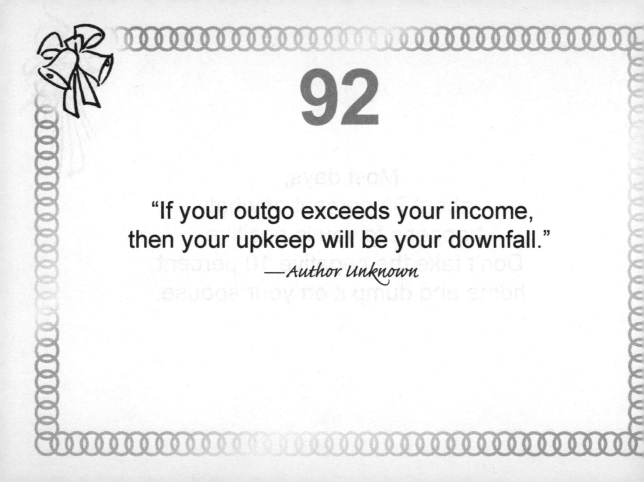

92

"If your outgo exceeds your income,
then your upkeep will be your downfall."

—*Author Unknown*

93

"Marry a person you love to talk to.
As you get older,
their conversation skills will be as
important as any other."

—*Author Unknown*

94

To have a happy marriage,
you must think "we"
more than you think "me."

95

Make sure you have
an understanding about
the "Big 3" before you
walk down the aisle—
money, children, and religion.

96

"Woman who beef too much
find herself in stew."

—*Author Unknown*

*What we have in
our hearts shows
on our faces.*

97

No matter how busy you get,
save at least two nights a month
for date nights, especially after the
babies start arriving.

98

Whoever said,
"grow old along with me—the best is yet to be,"
must have truly loved.

99

You've made your plans,
thought everything through.
Now it's time to put them into practice.
Are you ready?
The wedding is just the beginning.
Keep growing and learning.

JUST MARRIED

100

"If you live to be a hundred,
I want to live to be a hundred minus one day
so I never have to live without you."

—*Winnie the Pooh*

None of us know how many days we have.
Treasure each one as if it's your last.

101

*(Write your own most important
piece of advice for the newlyweds.)*

_____

_____

_____

_____

_____

_____

_____

(Write your own most important
piece of advice for the newlyweds.)

Many special thanks to:

Whitney Butler, Keith Blackmon, Andrea Lovejoy, Connie Mansour, Dale Mallory, Jean Park, Dave Norris, Stuart Gulley, Jim Thornton, Alecia Wheeler Clamp, Glenda Major, Jimmy Morgan, Marlene Wheeler, Susan Ferguson, Dr. Harold Lawrence, Nancy Durand, Darlene Stephens, Cindy Jackson, Becky Major, Jan Oliver, Sandy Cox, Susan Ducote, Ashley McWhorter, Lari Steed, Buddy Cashwell, Bobby Carmichael, Nadine Abbott, Todd Willis, Kim Adams, Laura Jennings, Sherri Brown, Pam Vaughn, Roxie (who never left my side), Meredith and Anna who are my inspiration, and to all who have shared their wisdom with me knowingly or unknowingly.

101

Most Important Things You Need to Know Before You Graduate

Life Lessons You're Going to Learn Sooner or Later . . .

RENAE WILLIS

Also
Now
Available

Wherever
Books Are
Sold

1-4165-4982-X

HOWARD BOOKS
A DIVISION OF SIMON & SCHUSTER